Reading Between The Lines

by

Vic Millington

SPIEGL PRESS

Published by Spiegl Press
6, St. George's Street, Stamford, Lincs. U.K.

Printed by Peter Spiegl & Co.,
6, St. George's Street, Stamford, Lincs. U.K.

ISBN 0 902544 70 5

FOREWORD

by

Paul Atterbury FRSA

I first met Vic Millington about ten years ago, when I was exploring the Cornish branch lines for my book, *See Britain By Train*. On duty as a guard that day on the Falmouth branch, he found my spread of maps and notebooks sufficiently unusual to engage me in conversation. He told me about his life, revealing that he was not only a railway enthusiast, but also an established railway painter. Later, we arranged to meet at Par station and he took me to his home, where I greatly enjoyed his paintings, his railway memorabilia and what must have been the shortest garden railway in Britain.

Vic is a remarkable man, a thorough going railwayman in the traditional mould, who has dedicated his life to what used to be an honourable profession. While occupied as a signalman, guard, roster clerk or in other railway activities, he has been a great observer of the passing scene. He also has an insatiable curiosity about people, many of whom come to life in these pages.

The enthusiasm of railways, a curiously British phenomenon, is widespread, affecting all ages and all levels of society. Vic's memories underline this enthusiasm in a most pertinent and entertaining way because railways are, after all, about people.

HIPS CHANDLE

NEW YEAR'S EVE

Tonight it's New Year's Eve. The last of the old snow crunches underfoot on the sleepers, grubby, with melt-holes like crotchetwork under the lineside trees. A mist hangs on the meadow and halos around the neon lights by the level crossing, tem-perature hovers just above the zero. The streets are deserted.

In steam days, at midnight, the night shift loco-shed workers would be out in the yard giving the whistles hell, if there was sufficient steam still available at this late hour. Along Dock Lane the ships' engineers on watch would do likewise, and any shipping out in the coastal waters would reply with a blast of their hooters. It was rather a pleasant cacophony, along with the church bells ringing from distant parishes.

Last time I went down to the harbour on New Year's Eve at midnight in diesel days, only the shipping and churches made any attempt to celebrate, along with a bunch of young revellers. I did see Samantha though, leaning out of a porthole window, naked as a new born, obviously celebrating. The trouble with Samantha is she is not very domesticated and once the elastic had failed in her undergarments she became hapless and often wayward. Although she cannot be likened to the wise virgins and their lamps, at least she is prepared for anything the incoming tides throw at her!

HOT BOX

Willy 'phoned yesterday to say that Dave Davies had gone on. A mountain of a man, big in the Union, too. Like a lot of the old footplate men for years he had had a part-time job, as a window cleaner, to help make ends meet when his family were growing up.

I liked old Dave, though he put the wind up me one night, back along. They'd been putting in modern signalling through Petermouth, where we passed through on a night freight job. 'Twas winter and a foul night and the poor handsignalmen were having a hard time of it, clipping and cranking all the points as they set up each train's route manually. Now running very late, I 'phoned our destination yard to tell the shunter not to hang about any longer for us, but to push off home. Grateful, he told me which road our return traffic was stabled in, and said he's laid a fire in the brake van.

Eventually we arrived, and I cut off our loco from the inwards' traffic, dropped down onto our back-working and coupled up. I walked the length of the train, examining it as I went, until I arrived at the van on the stop blocks. I lit the three lamps and the stove, and perused our load forms left on top of the locker. The train was standing in an old platform road, and both sides were obstructed by sleepers and Permanent Way materials. I only had my handlamp and it was dark as a sack in the pouring rain with a gale blowing - not even a rat about. I hurried along the other side of the train on the platform to advise the driver of his load, said that I was ready when he was, and made my way back to the van. No sooner had I sat down when the couplings snatched and we were on our way. I exchanged hand signals with Dave. Out of the old yard we rumbled, up to the exit signal. It was then that I observed sparks flying from one wagon in the middle of the train. In order to alert the driver, I turned the nearside side-lamp around to show red forwards, and cranked the handbrake on and off, on and off, to try and attract Dave's attention. But he never looked back once!

We passed relatively quickly through Petermouth this time, by the power signal box to where all the hand-signalmen had returned for supper, as our's was the last train. I flashed a red handsignal in all directions, but no-one was looking out from any-where. Now it was customary for the driver to always look back when we passed the big iron bridge over the river, to see that his train was following correctly. But not tonight! Dave was keeping his head dry, and opened up the loco to try and recover lost time. It was twenty miles before we passed the first manual signal box where thankfully the bobby saw my red hand signal and stopped us at his intermediate home signal. In the depths of the countryside's darkness I scrambled along the ballast spilt onto the cess to the defective wagon, and found that I'd missed a handbrake pinned down in the middle of the train on what had been the platform side in the train yard. I unpinned the brake lever and placed it on its rest, as the rain spat and hissed on the hot steel wheelsets. I went forward to tell Dave what the problem was, and when we eventually set off again, two sets of eyes peered towards the middle of the train where an old LMS three-plank clanked along with flat tyres for the remainder of the journey.

Needless to say, the vehicle was green-carded at our destination. For two days, my arms ached from having cranked the handbrake on and off for a full half hour.

Signalbox!

NIGHT RATE

The depot had several men who were brothers and sons, a legacy from the old days when successive generations followed on in the same occupation. Dave Davies had a brother, Eric, a guard, who was just as small as Dave was big. He was a very good gardener and his dahlias and bean rows were a joy to behold. During the winter, when the north-easterlies dragged in great heaps of seaweed, he'd be down there on the flats bagging up for his garden. By coincidence his wife Sally was born on the same day that he was.

Now if they have a fault it is their drinking, though they have good enough reason I suppose, having lost two children in separate accidents. He is a proper character, and has the gift of starting an argument in the pub then disappearing down the road to the next hostelry. Many a time before drinking was prohibited on or before duty I've seen him staggering into the depot. On one of the last night-ballast trains I worked he was booked to relieve me, top of the depot yard outside the signal box. As 01.30 approached, I tidied up the brake van, filled the stove up until its bottom glowed red with heat, and went out onto the veranda to see if he was coming down the Dock Main.

This train yard was well lit compared with some in the district, but then only by 60 watt bulbs at the top of forty foot poles. Now running very late, he stumbled across the trackwork underfoot and eventually arrived to relieve me. Seeing what state he was in, I sat him in the ducket, made him comfortable, put his tea can on the stove and left him to it.

I left the van and made for the foreman's office to ask why on earth he'd allowed Eric to book on in such a state. Now it became apparent that Fatherless Foreman had booked him on duty like it because it was cheaper to pay him just nightrate than me rest-day worked on night shift. Anybody would think that Fatherless was paying us out of his own pocket.

Advent Wooding

GLUTTON

Another pair of brothers who both worked on the footplate and were as different as chalk and cheese were Burt and Lou Cooper. They could be very kind and also very cantankerous. Burt was very fat and he was renowned for his flatulence, up and down the line. No matter what he touched, Burt was a glutton. The railway doctor told him to lose six stones and gave him a diet sheet. Proud as punch, I'm working with him on the following day, and it is lunch time. Into the cabin he comes, me right behind, he sounds a fanfare and sits down. He opens up his big black driver's bag and produces two Tuppaware boxes. He quickly empties the first one, consisting of Ryvita, cottage cheese and yoghurt. "Well done Burt" I said. Straightaway he opens the other box and eats a large pasty. "What ARE you doing?" says I. "Well the doctor says I must eat Ryvita on my diet, so I did, then I ate my pasty."

On days in early Advent, we often went 'wooding' whenever it was possible, gathering logs for the Christmas season. We'd choose a quiet day, when traffic was light, and stop amongst the willows and sycamores and start felling, hardly so much as you'd notice from any one tree, environmentally friendly, over a large area. Burt would pack his cab so full he could hardly move, then he would use the verandahs and platform ends of the brake van, lashing the three foot lengths (handy car boot size) together with binder twine. That was okay, I suppose, but I often picked up my motorcycle at the first passenger station and would drop it off at the last before the depot, to save time waiting for the train home. There was just room, if you turned the handlebars, to stand it on the verandah. It was a bit hair-raising, however, if you were turned into the loop line at Stop All Junction, because leaving the far end of the loop was like a switchback and the bike would try to leap off its stand. I would have some explaining to do - 'Guard's Motorcyle Found on the Main Line' - I can just see it in the weekly newspaper!

STOP HALL JUNC

WILLY

Burt's brother Lou was a lay preacher, or part-time saint. He could be very awkward, especially when he had a strop on with Fatherless Foreman, he would never then get a move on, but hang the pot, and he had a reputation for being exceedingly slow.

One summer Saturday Willy Waters and I were booked to work one of those holiday trains from London to the coast. We didn't get many chances to work four bells down the main, so we liked to make an impression. When we booked on, Fatherless Foreman (whose nickname was Ludo) advised us that our express was twenty minutes down entering the county. Willy and I walked across the branch loop to wait for our train in the main line platform. After a quick crew change, I gave Willy the green flag and we rocketed away up the bank. I was busy doing a ticket inspection in the train and conscious Willy was doing his best to make up lost time - he gave us an exhilarating ride to put it mildly. At the second big station we arrived almost on time, having made up the best part of twenty minutes in twenty-five miles. Down the platform comes the chief steward, a middle-aged cockney.

"Here guard, what's your 'kin driver's name?" he asks.

"What's the problem?" says I.

"He's 'kin well knocked all the spirits off the top shelf and 'kin well broken the lot, he's going too hard".

"I'm sorry" says I, "I'll go an ask him."

Arms on his hips in his white jacket, he stands and watches me walk down the length of the train to the loco.

"Hello driver" says I to Willy, "can you give me your name please, the Chief Steward says you've broken all his spirit bottles and he's going to report you."

Willy, with a twinkle in his eye, replies "tell him my name is Cooper, Lou Cooper."

So I walked back down to my van where 'white coat' was still standing with his arms on his hips, and told him what Willy had said. After this small delay we duly set off and arrived at destination right time. We never heard any more about this incident. 'Twas funny, but whenever there was an incident with the buffet staff, it was always the bottles from the top shelf that got broken!

LUDO I

Ludo, the Fatherless Foreman, was aware of his nickname, though you never used it directly in front of him. Years ago, he had had a donkey cart, and on one particular day, Ludo, his donkey, took off alone down Truck Hill leaving Fatherless behind. It became the joke of the winter amongst the depot's traincrews, and thereafter he himself was known as 'Ludo'.

It so happened that Ludo and Willy had, in their younger days, been mates, and had gone to a village dance on pushbikes up hill and several miles away, but fell out over a maiden and hated each others' guts for the next forty years. Ludo could be a very shrewd character when it suited, sometimes to your advantage, too. During a busy period there would be specific loaded wagons at various locations in the district that needed to be taken to the docks, and the empties returned for reloading urgently, more trips in excess of what your shift diagram advertised. The carrot Ludo dangled as an incentive to get more work from the traincrew was - as soon as you shifted these wagons you could go home! That meant we tried to cram eight hours work into six hours whenever possible. It was a system that worked well, and was known as being 'given a journey', because our customers were happy, the loco was back on shed and could then be utilised for other work, and the train-crew went up the road in good time. Of course to achieve this, you needed the co-operation of all the Signalmen, who got nothing out of it because their shifts were eight hours anyway and some resented our dashing about the district, forgoing meal breaks and very probably interrupting theirs. You needed to reassure the Bobby who the Driver was too, say Willy or someone reliable, who would not let them down when they gave you the road in front of a passenger train. If you had Lou Cooper up front, you never had a chance, because from the start of the shift he would try to make overtime by hang-ing about.

Ludo had always been a schemer before his promotion to Foreman. He'd been a Driver at our depot and therefore knew all the moves and tricks that locomen got up to, to make overtime or skive.

LUDO II

One summer Saturday afternoon Ludo and I were working on the seaside branch and our D.M.U. was playing up - only two of the four engines were working. I said from the start that we'd never make it out of the parish. Loaded down to the gunwales with incoming holidaymakers already tired and irritable with their children, dogs and luggage in the heat, having changed from a main line train, they fought for seats in the airless train. Again I spoke to Ludo and said that we'd never make it and he replied "We shall get around the corner up the bank near to the emergency 'phone and there we shall fail. We'll hang around for five minutes whilst I try to restart, then you can 'phone the bobby, tell him we've failed and cannot go on up the bank because we only have two engines but, if he will authorise us to set back downhill we can make it back to the station. By the time we get there, the Birmingham will be knocking and we'll have lost our paths. We shall be asked to take the unit to shed for fitter's attention, but by the time Dick's had a look I shan't have enough time to make our last trip because my day will be up and I'm not making overtime today. He'll tell us to sit in the cab for an hour, then send us home.

And that was exactly what happened. Ludo didn't care about the inconvenience to our passengers, who eventually arrived at the resort an hour or so later than planned. It was pointless arguing with him; like a lot of the old steam men they thought they were some sort of god, anyway.

CAUSE AND EFFECT

In the Autumn, come September month, freight for the docks would increase twofold for a couple of weeks and there would be a rush to get loaded to the quayside and empties back to the works between the tides. And the reason for all this was an ocean away - literally the Atlantic Ocean, for in the next few weeks the St. Lawrence Seaway would be freezing up and all shipping halted there for the winter. Sometimes the local branch passenger train would be delayed for a minute or two because of the extra freight traffic, but the passengers usually took it in good faith when you explained the reason.

On one such day, tired and weary after overtime on a busy morning freight, I walked up the lane to my cottage, put the leash on the dog and took him for a walk to the paper shop, tying him up outside. After buying my paper I returned home, had a cup of tea and then got between the sheets for an hour before the children came home from school. "Where's Punch gone?" was the next thing I remember, all puddin' headed. "I don't know" I replied, "he was here when I came home."

We set off separately to search the neighbourhood. No Punch! Then Mrs Gossip Garter, the shunter's wife from down the lane came up the path and knocked on the door to announce:

"What's you dog doing tied up outside the paper shop. He's been there for ages!"

Retired...

ENDOWMENTS

My mate Willy had two large endowments in life. The first he was born with, of which the least said the better! The second he came by.

Like a lot of the old footplate men, he had done a bit of part-time farming and gardening in the 'fifties to help ends meet. One old lady he had looked after eventually died and left him a quarter of a million in money, property and investments. Despite this, he didn't alter one bit, in fact he still rolls his own cigarettes and plays Bingo an Friday and Sunday nights, and his wife Lily still bakes the best pasties in the county.

It was for the former endowment for which he was famous and not a little unproud, nor shy on a good day. Several times I've seen him shunting on the Yard Pilot on a hot summer's day, standing in the loco cab doorway sunbathing it, bumping into stationary wagons allowing it to swing about.

It was the only loco at out depot that sported three vacuum pipes!

LAMP MAN

It's not that long since practically every location had an oil-house, and there are still many about in areas of manual signal boxes. The wells of signal lamps last eight days, and the old oil tail lamps, with their smaller reservoirs, several days. Usually they have a stone or concrete floor, damp and stained with paraffin, which is stored in forty gallon drums, and trigged up on a wooden trestle. It needs two of you to set up a fresh drum, first you upend it, unscrew the bung and exchange the tap off the empty barrel, then it is manhandled into position on the trestle ready for use. As the tap usually drips, inevitably a galvanised bucket is to be found at the business end of the drum.

On the shelves in the oil house various spares, wicks, reservoirs and burners clutter together, with Brasso, steel wool, feeder cans and, in former days, bundles of brightly coloured cotton waste for mopping up spilt oil and polishing the glasses of the lamps. The door inevitably sports a 'Smoking Prohibited' sign. Always, the smell of paraffin hangs in the air, sometimes known as kerosene or lamp oil.

A good lampie regularly cleans the lenses and lamp glasses and polishes the reflectors of the lamps in his care. The brass burners flip off and polish up handsome with Brasso, although sometimes you need a penknife to scrape off the tar that can build up with use. The top of the wick often needs pinching off and trimmed level with a pair of scissors, and when relighting you need to let the flame settle before you can adjust it so that it does not smoke. Some lamp glasses have markers engraved on them to help with setting the flame. Then the lamp is usually blown out until it is needed. Each signal on the lampie's patch has a regular day for changing once a week, hence the eight day capacity of the reservoirs.

All the signals, if not the direct vision of the bobby, have to have indicators, consisting of a bi-metallic strip, fitted in their chimneys. Should the lamp fail, the strip cools, and an indicator or buzzer is energised and alerts the signalman of the failure. Trying to relight a lamp in a gale atop a signal post is a work of art in itself.

STORAGE
5
10
15
20
25
30
0
lb/in²
LMS
DERBY

STREET WISE

In the early days of railway history, new towns sprung up around villages at important junctions. To house the large numbers of railway staff at these locations, the old companies often erected narrow streets of terraced cottages straggling along cobbled roads, that they rented out. By the late 'fifties and early 'sixties they were getting more and more run down and neglected, and they were sold off relatively cheaply and occupied by those unable to afford anything more substantial during this period of their lives. Some areas became even rougher and more deprived therefore.

One pair of old-style locomen who worked together regularly for years and were more like father and son provide the next yarn.

The driver, older and more experienced, kidded his younger mate on something terrible and told him he wouldn't be a 'real man' until he'd had a 'close' relationship with a member of the opposite sex. With this the younger man had had no success. So one evening his mentor lent him his car and gave him a fiver and told him to go and find a willing partner, who resided in such deprived areas.

Driving slowly down a narrow street, he saw a young lady in a short skirt, dyed blond hair, sporting a red shoulder handbag. Thinking he was perhaps lost she beckoned to him and asked if he was in-terested in doing any business. Red faced, he replied how much would the venture cost. About some things in life he was streetwise, so when she said five pounds he knocked her down to two, to which she apparently agreed. That now left him with a predicament, he only had a five pound note that his mate had given to him and he daren't now risk asking for change, so on the way he called at the station kiosk and bought some cigarettes and kept the change for himself. It seems I'm told, the business was completed in no time at all, he bade farewell to his guide and returned the car to his mate. Obviously now embarrassed, his mate had sufficient tact not to question him at this time, it would wait until tomorrow....

Over the first cup of tea that day, the young man had to recount the full story. The older driver laughed when the youngster confessed he'd kept his socks on, though nothing else, because he didn't want to risk catching a verruca!

140

PASSENGER AND FREIGHT TRAIN INSTRUCTIONS.

GRAM SHOWING CLASSIFICATION, HEAD LAMPS AND CORRESPONDING BELL SIGNALS—*continued.*

Head Lamps. (White Lights.)	Description of Trains.	Beats on Bell.	How to be Given.
	Empty Coaching Stock train not specially authorised to carry " A " headlamps ..	5	2 pause 2 pause 1.

Empty Stock

JACKPOT

Now the younger locoman had obviously benefitted from this experience, and was now filled with a new confidence in his attitude towards the fair sex. So much so, in fact, that one evening the following summer, when he was working with Willy on the seaside branch, he found the courage to impress even him!

The resort was full of visitors and late on, as dusk fell, the pair decided to go for a pint and some chips. As they went into the bar, Willy gave the youngster a pound note and told him to get the beer in whilst he went onto the one-armed bandit. As usual, Willy was lucky and won the jackpot at his second attempt. The locals glared at him, but he wasn't worried by them, just smiled, flashing his dentures.

"Drink up" he said, "we'll make time for another."

So they did, and then set off for the chip shop around the corner. The younger man only had a ten shilling note on him, so he bought fish and chips for Willy and a large bag of chips for himself.

Time was going by and they were now walking own the station road eating their supper, when two young ladies approached from the opposite direction. One obviously took a fancy to the youngster and asked him:

"Please may I have a chip?"

Now I did say that he was streetwise, and filled with a new confidence, so much so that he replied:

"OK. A chip for a handful?"

Apparently she was delighted and helped herself to his chips whilst the youngster helped himself to a very large handful.

"Come on" said Willy, "we're late already."

So they hurried off into the station, having had an eventful meal break. Needless to say, the train arrived right-time at the junction!

My last shunt with steam!

TOUPEE

When I was comparatively young my hair started to recede and I bought a toupee, with which I had some fun. It cost me £80 back then! The foreman shunter, Don Cheddar, a bit older and even balder than me, used to borrow it on Saturday evenings to wear when he got dressed up to go to the Railwaymen's Club.

Even on hot summer days, on passenger work, you were expected to wear your full uniform, including your hat. My head would roast under all that lagging of both hat and wig, but I learned to use it to advantage sometimes, if there was a child upset on the journey. Whilst checking tickets, if I came across such an upset youngster, I would first remove my hat, then lift the front portion of the toupee and scratch my bald head. That would immediately stop the tears and their eyes would nigh pop out of their sockets.

When I first started wearing it I was naturally a bit self-conscious. One day, whilst shunting in the factory yard with Stephen Derrick, usually a very pleasant well mannered driver, I was riding on the loco step as we approached the ingoing siding. It was rather windy. First my uniform hat blew off, followed by my toupee (you stick them on with special double-sided tape). Of course, Stephen happened to see the whole performance and just had to say something, instead of feigning to look the other way.

"Catch the cat" he called as my toupee cartwheeled away, borne on the wind, round and round it went, and eventually died right in the middle of a filthy puddle.

I recovered both my hat and my hairpiece, shook them, and replaced them like a lid on a jam jar as though it was an everyday occurrence, trying to save my composure, but my face was red with embarrassment, right in front of Gossip Garters shunter-husband, too!

IRON ORE
TIPPLER

DENTURES

Another recovery job almost as embarrassing was when I was out with the local flatulence club; Burt (the glutton) Cooper and Colin Vines. We had been to the Railway Staffs' Annual Handicrafts Exhibition, and on the way home changed trains, and whilst we were waiting went into the railway buffet for a sandwich and a pint. Burt was not content with just a sandwich, he had to go down the road and bring back a double portion of fish and chips, and sat down in the buffet to eat them.

"You can't do that in here" said Colin, "they'll throw us all out."

Time and beer quickly passed, and it was nearly time to catch our train home.

"I don't feel so good" said Colin, and went down the platform to the Gents. I thought it best to follow him and make sure he was alright. Hell, you've never heard anything like it! Colin in the cubicle was bellowing like a bull from both ends! An old boy came in to use the toilet, looked aghast, and quickly finished his business.

"Hell" shouts Colin. "I've just lost my false teeth down the loo!" And then he promptly flushed it...

Drastic action was called for, so I found the manhole cover outside the toilet, lifted it up and waited for the teeth (amongst other things) to appear. I managed to fish them out, ran back into the loo, and washed them under the cold water tap. Having relieved his discomfort, Colin unlocked the door and reappeared, very red faced. I thrust his teeth back at him and told him to put them into his mouth, and he did so without realising. An hour later he asked:

"Where on earth did you find my teeth?"

I avoided a direct answer and said:

"It doesn't matter as long as you got them back."

Never again did he mention his teeth, and neither did I until today, but he never seemed to have had any ill effects from the episode.

BR

TAIL LAMPS

Tail lamps were always a problem at our depot. In the early mornings the night trains would return with empties, fuel oil, seed tatties, gunpowder and coal, that had come long distances as full load trains, from Scotland and the Midlands. On arrival in our yard, the shunting staff would re-form them into shorter trains for local trip workings in our district. Therefore more trains went away from the yard than arrived, causing an imbalance in tail lamps. Some guards would have secret hoards and pick them up from other locations to replace the deficiencies.

I got caught once though. After the engine was coupled up, a brake test performed, a lamp would be placed on the bracket at rear, prior to leaving the yard. Sometimes it was necessary to refill its well and wipe the lens and reflector and trim and relight the wick. I was waiting on the loco for the bobby to give us the road, and along came Cockney Twinkle, apparently late for duty as usual, and nicked my tail lamp. I was not aware of this until the signalman reported me for not having a red lamp on the end of the train.

Sometimes the overnight freights would be very late getting home, and especially during the winter months the train crews would stay in the warmth of the cabin by the old coal stove, drinking tea, playing rummy, telling yarns, or trying to sleep on the long hard benches.

One form of initiation for a young guard was to carry a tail lamp on his endowment. It was a very painful gesture that would bring a tear to the eye, for you had to parade your prowess in front of the men in the cabin. They'd seen it all before though, and usually poured out a cup of strong stale tea for the exhibitionist afterwards.

NO
SMOKING

BLACK OIL

The lamp man is at the bottom of the pay scale and in the past was the first post of a new entrant took before promotion, more often than not. Sometimes a green-carded man - if he was permitted still to work by the line and able to climb the ladders - was glad to hold this position. Signal lamps stay lit, day and night, and many's the time I've done lamping as part of overtime duties. Should a lamp fail by night, the signalman next in rear of the failure has to stop and caution all trains, warning them of the failure, thus causing delays. Many's the time I've made a shilling after a shift and gone out to relight a lamp. Sometimes the bobby would report that his Outer Home signal was full of 'black oil' - in other words - extinguished. On the branch lines you often gave the lampie a lift to the distant signals, some three quarter miles away from the signal box, stopping for him to perform his work, or even volunteering to change the lamps yourself, on freight trips.

At some locations the regular signalmen do their own lamping, sharing this overtime duty with their mates. They would often assemble several lamps actually in the box, lighting them up before going out to change them. This would give the flames a chance to settle. If the flame was too high it smoked, and for hours afterwards little black smuts would drift around, usually to settle in your teacup! A good lampie wiped the bull's eye lens of the lamp case and the aspects, but not the signal arm, that is the signal department's duty when they service the signal, oiling up the moving parts.

Many staffed stations had a spare tail lamp to hand, or a can of paraffin, in case the bobby next in rear reported that a train's tail light was out, so that it could be replenished when it arrived in their platform. Some guards carried a small screw top bottle of paraffin with them in their satchels, in case of emergency, or to light a fire in the stove of a brake-van if it had not been prepared ready. The tail lamp, as you will probably know, is the confirmation that the train has arrived with all its vehicles intact - and therefore vital for safety - before a following train can be permitted to enter the other end of the section.

Railway signals are capable of displaying Red/ Yellow and Green aspects. If a signal becomes defective it is so constructed that the balance weight will return the signal to danger, should a signal wire break. The glasses in the spectacles are therefore Red, or Yellow and BLUE, which appears as Green when the yellow lamp behind it is seen. It's surprising how many modellers and artists paint these spectacles the wrong colour.

The lampie usually resented the intrusion of the guards in facilities they shared at some locations because they would leave the floor swimming in paraffin, or empty the drum and not report it to the foreman. A good lampie kept his work bench, consisting of a metal covered surface over timber, like a drawing board, relatively clean for safety purposes. In steam days, inevitably the loco crew would draw their lamps or lamp oil from their stores before they took the engine off shed.

I have spoken at length about oil and oil lamps. The railway did, until comparatively recently (and still does on some lines) rely heavily on humble paraffin - being a relatively cheap and portable fuel - for use at remote locations, especially.

"Put the kettle on,
Station Manager's on her way."

FACILITIES

Little consideration was given to train crews when it came to toilet facilities. Steam engines with a tender often provided a private corner. Tank engines and diesels were more of a problem, although some diesel engines have a basic urinal, akin to a drinking fountain, made of stainless steel, situated in the depths of the engine room. It calls for a measure of dexterity to find them, hidden behind lots of plumbing, and a work of art to use them when the loco is on the move. The guard in the van was worse off, though sometimes an old bucket could be found in the coal locker if he was lucky. Otherwise, all trainmen had to stand in the doorway and wrestle with the wind, waiting for a suitable rural location first, of course.

Fernley Philpot, a shunter on one of the branches, was a 'private' sort of person. Short, dumpy and middle-aged, you always knew when he was going to pass water, for he would shut himself out on the guard's van veranda, and whistle the same tune. He was a Plymouth Brethren, so it was naturally a hymn tune. The way he wrestled with two hands you thought he was a big lad, but always, on the step afterwards, there would be a damp patch. Of course you never dared say anything to him about it!

Somewhere I have a photograph of Fernley with the driver Burt (the glutton) in the woods. Fernley stands there immaculate in his uniform with his shoes shining. Behind, the guard has momentarily dropped his trousers around his ankles for the picture, whilst Burt is posed with a cast iron 18" frying pan, full of fishcake for his lunch.

Some six months later Fernley brought his wife along for a ride on the branch line. Needless to say, the driver showed her this photograph during a break for tea, near to the weir. Fernley had not been aware, until this moment, that the guard was in such a state of undress! She laughed, of course, but all he could do was say "Dear, dear" and shuffled off, flashing his white teeth, set off even more by a redder than usual pair of cheeks. Poor old Fernley!

ROYAL

It is always the senior top link men that are diagrammed to work the Royal Train, and we had several visits by Royalty during the course of most years. Often the whole train would stable on a country branch line overnight during its hours of closure, so that the party on board had a quiet night's rest before the following day's engagements.

Security was always very tight, spaced at suitable locations in its vicinity, and we had to bring along our photo I.D. cards to show we were bona-fide as we approached. Whilst I was in the junior link I was always in awe of the men selected, who would always turn up in their best uniforms and polished shoes. The Queen would send £5 tips for all the traincrew afterwards, but I never received any such compliment from Prince Charles, Princess Diana or Prince Michael when I worked their trains in later years. The train itself has its own on-board crew of dedicated staff. When you worked this train you were entitled to receive a Royal Train tie after five occasions.

In the early years of their fairytale marriage, I took a lot of photographs of Princess Di at one location, much to the consternation of one Palace official who told me in no uncertain terms to desist. However, I had a nod and wink from one of our own senior local railway inspectors to carry on 'pressing the shutter' as he wanted some copies himself!

The brake van at one end of the train is extremely comfortable and well appointed, but the other end is standard sized, with the generator set providing power for the lighting and air-conditioning in the parcel portion which is very noisy when it is running, and that, combined with the toilet pans that are stacked in the corner when not in situ under the coach ends, makes it hardly a 'des res'.

EMERGENCY

Several of the train crew had reputations for their encounters, often illicit, with the fair sex. Don Cheddar, who borrowed my toupee, was often up to some mischief or other, comforting a mate's spouse or mistress.

One sultry summer evening he was demonstrating this facet of his personality to a maiden by Carpenter's shop - near to where Ludo's D.M.U. failed that I wrote about earlier - on the bank in the woods. It was too hot and sticky under the trees to stay in the stuffy car so, naked, they wandered like Adam an Eve to find a shady hollow where they could lie. Unfortunately, when they returned to the vehicle Don realised he had left his car keys in his pocket, now locked inside. He was left with no alternative but to use the emergency railway phone and tell the foreman of his predicament.

Fortunately the foreman was in a sympathetic mood and found empathy in his heart, and was able to summon a train crew who had just returned to shed. He found a couple of long dust coats and sent them on the loco up the valley - 'to examine the line' - the bobby wrote in his Train Register, and rescued the embarrassed couple, bringing Don back home to find his spare set of car keys!

New set of overalls!

JUNCTION

Driver Eric Joshua also had a reputation for being fast and safe with both locomotives **and** ladies. I recall one night in the Autumn that after work he had gone home for tea, then took his black labrador dog for a walk. Pre-arranged, as the first stars were appearing in the eastern sky, he met his illicit partner by the gate on the path in the lane near to my cottage.

Unfortunately, the dog got bored and wandered off in the gloaming, eventually making his way back home, arriving a full half hour before Eric. He had some explaining do to when he himself arrived home to an anxious wife.

"Oh there he is" he said, "I've been looking everywhere for him" and then kicked the dog.

He was one of our better drivers, and fast, but you didn't feel unsafe or uncomfortable. He had a part-time decorating business for years with Don Cheddar, to help ends meet. He had one fatality though when I was a signalman at the Junction, when the shunter there was killed in the train yard whilst shunting. Clarence was a very kind soul, a Methodist, with a fine grown-up family, indeed his daughter was a G.P. Three of us worked the Junction between us, along with relief staff.

Three months before poor Clarence was killed I had another shock there. My oppo, Ken, had a heart attack and died in the box on duty. He was still laid across the frame when I got there, as the doc had been and certified him gone, but we were to wait for the undertaker. I moved him clear of the lever frame so that we could signal the branch passenger, closed his eyes, using old pennies to keep them shut, and covered his face with a clean lever cloth. After they took him away, I emptied his sandwich box for the birds and took it home after duty to his poor wife. After these incidents the Junction was always a sad place for me.

Though I work several hundred miles away these days, only last week did I hear the block bell ring at the Junction, as my old mate Dave phones me up occasionally, and long with Willy, keeps me up to date with the news.

I worked with Eric on his last day before retirement, after putting in forty odd years. We were working on a branch and Eric was having problems with the D.M.U. So much so that Ludo the foreman asked us to bring it back at lunch time instead of riding home on the cushions after our shift. We managed to persuade the bobby to give us the road in front of the stopper and after being assured that Eric was the driver he let us run. We came up like a bat out of hell. A mile from the Junction for the depot Eric announced:

"You know, we shall pass the home signal if it is on, don't you, there's no way I can stop her now in time with the vacuum all in, on a down hill gradient?"

It was on, and we passed it at walking pace and came to a stand in front of the signal box where Officer Dibble, a part-time Special Constable, was looking out of the window. Now Dibble knew it was Eric's last journey, so he just shook his head in disgust and pulled off for us to go to shed; for-tunately not mentioning that he had committed a 'cardinal sin' in the Train Register. Doubtless he would have been obliged to if it had been the previous week, before Eric retired.

LOWESBY
LOWESBY

RELIEF

Officer Dibble became a good friend over the years and loved to tell yarns about the old days. I did upset him one day though, when I had not been out working trains for very long.

Whilst standing outside his signal box waiting for the road one morning, I nipped up to make a can of tea. After refilling the kettle and putting it back on the stove, I swung the tea can around over my head, like all the trainmen did, but I forgot the low beams in the ceiling. The can crashed into the beam and emptied the boiling brew down my arm and then all over his highly polished floor. The hot liquid scalded my arm and removed the polish from the lino.

Signalmen take pride in their box interiors and it is common on Sunday mornings to re-polish the brown lino on the floor. Then every time that the signalmen change over, the man going home buffs it up and keeps it shining. One box on the Down line was particularly renowned for its polished floor. It was a busy Junction Box, but all the regular signalmen walked around with dusters on their shoes in skating fashion, polishing the floor as they attended to the lever frame throughout their shift.

Any trainman going into the box to sign the book, when he was detained there, had to stand on the door mat whilst the bobby brought the Train Register over to him. Woe betide him if he strayed off this mat!

About half an hour before the bobby changed over with his relief, it was common to see them walking down the wooden steps to empty the ashes and refill the coal bucket ready for the next man coming on duty. There is usually a set day in the week for cleaning the brasses and polishing the block bells too. Another Sunday morning chore, at the box where I was a signalman, was to empty the Elsan toilet bucket outside the railway fence onto the moor.

DOWN
UP
BR

BINGO!

The first derailment I was involved with and witnessed happened whilst I was out learning the road with the senior guard, Rick Boot. Although I had several mishaps over the subsequent twenty years, none of them fortunately were the result of my carelessness and I never was issued with a 'Form One' disciplinary warning.

On this first occasion, Morley Quinlocks was driving. He became a good friend but he had a short fuse and easily got excited. He liked a drop of lotion too. On the previous evening to this derailment he had been to the official opening of the Railwaymen's Club situated in the train yard behind the town's station. The following evening he was reversing a very long and heavy train uphill into this yard, in order to detach the rear portion. It was getting dark and because of obstructions and a reverse curve he was having difficulty observing the handsignals, but he knew by experience that he must be approaching the stop blocks, and working under a 'green' handsignal had reduced his speed to a snail's pace, feeling for the buffers as he went. Unfortunately, as soon as he touched them with the brake van they fell down like a domino-tower, the van did not even shudder but continued onwards, rolling across the tarmac and into the end wall of the very same Railwaymen's Club, where it demolished the wall, coming to rest in the room used as the cellar, just as its members were sitting down to Bingo. Morley then felt the resistance of his train and stopped, unable to see a handsignal, presumed he had touched the buffers. The brake van fractured the water and beer pipes, which proceeded to spurt out like the Tivoli Fountains! I couldn't help smiling and fortunately no one was hurt in the mishap.

The train guard detached the wagon destined for this location then, having moved the tail lamp forwards, 'phoned the foreman to tell him of the derailment, then called the bobby and got the road, and advised Morley of the mishap and his new train load. Morley refused to believe Rick's account of this further 'opening' of the Club and said "I've got bad nerves, you shouldn't say such things to me". It was not until we were back on the shed and the foreman asked Morley for a report form about the incident that he believed it!

He had spent such an enjoyable evening in the Railwaymen's Club twenty four hours previous, which he recounted when we first booked on duty. He said that because of the state in which he arrived home, his wife had made him sleep in the spare room. Unfortunately he had to get up to relieve himself during the night and forgot where he was and had one in the wardrobe!

The following morning I took my camera to the site to record the derailment. Soon afterwards I submitted it to the staff newspaper 'Rail News' and receiv-ed a cheque for £5 for sending it in.

1A16
THE
FLYING
SCOTSMAN

TOUCHED

Some time later I was shunting off my train very late at night, single handed, in the middle of the city. The weather was atrocious, a strong wind and with rain coming own like stair-rods. The yard's resident rabbits must have thought I was 'lamping' for them and were running about underfoot all over the place.

The driver, John Hoff, was a miserable old beggar at the best of times. The train was very heavy and the rear end at the foot of an incline. At the front end next to the loco were half a dozen tank wagons with AFI brakes. These wagons were very difficult, if not impossible, to shunt with, for as soon as the slightest brake application was made by the driver their brakes applied fully. A now disgruntled and wet John was leaning out of the cab obeying my hand-signals as we set back, pulled ahead, then set back into the various sidings. Progress down hill was like a pig with the trots, all or nothing, no intermediate slow speeds. John was setting back under a 'green' handsignal into an almost empty road and touched a lightweight empty Permanent-Way wagon that woke up into life like a startled cat, ran down the rest of the siding as if trying to escape and mounted the buffer stops, where it landed with its midships perilously perched atop of the wooden cross beam.

Next morning the resident shunter, a freemason like our boss, wasn't best pleased, neither was his father-in-law Jack, the carriage and wagon examiner. (Jack's daughter, Miriam - a nicer person you couldn't wish to meet - still works at the Travel Centre at this station).

For years and years life goes on seemingly without change, the same old faces at the same locations, but then in a relatively short space of time it all changes, especially when you move away yourself and get snippets of information periodically from old mates about old colleagues. John, the driver, was a tight old so and so, and apart from his wife had neither chick nor child to feed, yet for years and years he lived practically rent free in a nice bungalow in exchange for performing caretaking duties at the local Catholic church, and he also put in as many hours as was possible on the footplate.

NOT
TO BE
MOVED
FLYING SCOTSMAN

DUTY FREE

Another set of brothers were also on the footplate, Ned and Ben Cory, and goodness were they characters, both very eccentric, short in stature, intelligent with a good interest and knowledge of the county's industrial history, and would tell yarns for hours when you were working with them.

When Ned had been a fireman, his driver, one of the old Great Railwaymen, was an equal in character strength too. For a few shillings a week he looked after the heating system in the local chapel, cleaning the flues and chimney and during the winter lighting fires on cold Sunday mornings for the comfort of the congregation. One particular Sunday he achieved a longstanding ambition and got the chapel so hot by his efforts that the candles up front began to melt and bend in their brass holders. One can imagine the response of the Minister that morning...

Ned's brother, Ben, could be very moody and you never knew how to take him from one day to the next. He was an excellent gardener and one morning, after our early freight shift, he invited me to go home and see his garden. His vegetables were prizeworthy, in fact the whole plot was immaculate beyond criticism. He loaded me down with an armful of rhubarb and a tray of fresh eggs from his henhouse.

Lo and behold, the very next morning, on the same shift, he had a strop on and could only manage a grunt in response to any communication from me. After uncoupling from a train of loaded wagons, we drew ahead into the departure road onto a string of empties at the dockside. The dock shunters were very busy dealing with our inwards cargo that they were trying to berth on the quayside for unloading as the ship was due away on the next tide that was already on the flow. In their haste they had not fully prepared the empties and as I was checking I began to find many instanter couplings in the long position. I therefore returned to our loco to ask Ben to ease up the string of wagons onto the rear half a dozen that had their brakes pinned down, in order that I could shorten the couplings. Would he ease up? No! I had to wait for the dock engine to finish dealing with the inwards traffic before it could then squeeze the wagons up from the rear, thus considerably delaying our departure. Consequently we were then late arriving with the empties at our factory destination, whose loading bank staff were teasy with me because, as our foreman gave us a 'journey' so their captains would do the same thing. The sooner they loaded a given number of wagons, a greater number in a shorter time interval, they were allowed to go home. As a result, the next time you arrived at their siding and said you'd got a 'journey on' they would be uncooperative.

We didn't mind helping the dock shunters out a bit, even your driver would assist you preparing your train and taking numbers sometimes, to effect a prompt departure, because often there was the chance of a bit of duty free baccy or spirits that the steveores came by on the jetties. Isn't it funny, but a bit of duty free tastes so much better somehow?

TRUTH

You met many wonderful people, some quite famous, on the most mundane journeys sometimes. However one meeting left me cold in the knowledge of how small a world this can be and how truth will out, given time.

I had an old Aunt Agnes, my great aunt really, who went a bit senile at the end of her long life and talked about 'things' she had seen and heard, before she was put away into a home.

Some twenty years and three hundred miles later, I was departing from a seaside terminal with a stopping train, and was in the middle of a ticket check. It was out of season and very quiet on board, but quite often you found someone glad of a chat as you went about the train. I saw a kindly-faced middle-aged lady, who I deduced from her return ticket was actually on her way to the county of my birth. I commented on this and asked her where she was heading after the train arrived, telling her that I hailed from that place, originally.

She replied "Gypsy Lane - do you know it?"

"Quite well, I use to have an old aunt who lived there" I said.

"What was her name?"
"My poor old Aunt Agnes - but sadly she went senile in her last years."

"I used to live next door" she replied, "what do you mean she went senile?"

"Well" says I, clearing the tickle just arrived in my throat, "seeing things at her window, bangings on the wall...."

"But she DID" replied the lady, "I've seen the neighbours from the other side dressed in masks looking through the windows, and banging on the wall with a hammer, they were trying to drive her out."

What a coincidence! My poor old aunt was speaking to me indirectly from another place, after all the years that had passed and the miles, but in the end the truth of her unhappy ending came out!

BLIND

Whilst working the branch trains over the years we got to know many of the regulars and they got to know you by name. This promoted a very nice environment in which to travel and work, and if one of them was perhaps upset by some turn in life, a kind word never went amiss. You were privileged to look after young children left in your care by their mums for the first few days when starting at a new school. Sometimes you had to raid your sandwich box and find a Penguin to distract them when tearful. They never forgot you and having once established the habit of commuting by train, you watched them grow up all down the years, followed their progress to new schools, further education. You were introduced to their boy/girlfriends, got invited to weddings, christenings and funerals.

One little maiden stands out in my memory. Zoe, when she was about five, started travelling on the branch. I will always remember her first trip. It was rush hour at tea-time on a hot summer's day. I was sitting in the van having a quick pipe between trips when this slip of a girl came in and plonked herself down on the floor. She rubbed her hands across the hard surface and said aloud:

"That's funny, this floor is made of concrete."

She was apparently totally oblivious of my presence. Then I realised that she was completely blind.

"Hello" says I, "I am the train guard."

She came over towards me and said "What's a guard?"

I explained as best I could and gave her my uniform hat to examine.

"Phew" she said "it's a bit cheesy!

She played with the hat and my guard's whistle, and then it was time to depart so I took her back to her mum.

Soon afterwards she became a regular on Monday mornings and Friday tea-time trains, going to a special school, accompanied by an escort, for several years. Often, when I had a quiet minute I would take her forwards into the driving compartment to say 'hello' to the driver. She soon learned where the horn control was located and would give it hell until her escort, embarrassed, would call her back into the train. She was a very pretty little girl with short red hair and gazelle-like long white legs, and she became everybody's favourite on the train. She once brought some photographs to show me of a party she'd been to and was in fancy dress, although obviously she couldn't see them herself. In one picture, exhausted by the day, there she is curled up like a doormouse in an easy chair, in a pretty flower fairy dress, fast asleep, with a headband of real primroses slipped down across her forehead.

I asked her once if she could see anything at all and she replied she could sometimes see the light of the sun if she stared at it. Sometimes she would rub her eyes excessively. Years later I found out that this is quite common to the blind, because in doing so little whisps of white light are stimulated by thus rubbing. The last I heard she was doing very well and had won medals for swimming and horse riding.

"We must stop doing this....."

INSTINCT

Years later, I moved away to a new location and worked on the platforms, and we had quite a lot to do with blind passengers who attended a special training unit nearby. Most of them were wonderful souls and were always pleased to receive a friendly voice when you met them from the trains and took them around to the taxi rank. We were advised by telex of their names, coach seat numbers and train times before their arrival by the Customer Services unit at Headquarters.

The chargeman at the station, Peter, was quite a formidable Sikh gentleman, very sober and strict, whose very presence commanded respect. In time he became a close and wonderful friend.

One day I escorted a coloured blind passenger from the train as usual, then returned to the office for a cup of tea that Peter had made. I remarked "How do you explain coloured and white people to the blind?"

After a pause, Peter replied "Instinct, they would sense a difference, not just because of different accents."

I thought for a long time afterwards about this and conjectured what it must be like to be blind and coloured, and how do you explain away prejudice and ignorance....?

STRANGERS

It was extremely satisfying work to be trusted by so many strangers. Often one of the quieter children, or one suffering the torment of a bully, would ask if they could sit with you in the van and get on with their homework, or just to seek refuge.

The boys could be very mischievous and you had to keep an eye on their pranks. Cockney Twinkle, the guard, got left behind at one station as one of the lads gave the driver 'right away' on the buzzer, and Cockney, embarrassed, had to summon a taxi to take him to the next station.

On odd days they wouldn't come near the van though, if you had a coffin on board, complete with its brass nameplate of the 'interned'. We never let on that it was empty as yet and we used to play the role - the station staff and myself - removing our hats as we loaded the box very reverently onto the train. One of the local undertakers would meet you at its destination and, tipping a wink, you carried on with the ceremony until the hearse was loaded!

One pretty young maid used to park herself in the van without being invited, to complete her prep on the morning train. Isabel was always busy and one day I asked her why of late she apparently was writing so much verse, which I could see were really love letters, trying to wind her up.

"They are love letters" she replied, "to someone very special."

Then she went on to confide in me that she had 'come out' and they were addressed to an older lady who worked in the Council Offices.

It was a shock to me, and for a moment I felt as any parent would, when their child announces that they are gay.

'Crib time'

MATCHMAKING

Some of the railway staff established quite involved relationships, often illicit, with the opposite sex, and eventually two mates married passengers.

On the back working of Zoe's train, in the mornings, three young lady students would travel with us to college. About this time, I had a very good mate, a second man, Luke Pears, about twenty years of age, very shy, blond-haired, with a very fresh complexion. He was a lovely lad, and lonely, so I asked him if he would like me to fix him up with a date. He was delighted and readily agreed, so I started my first bit of matchmaking!

I approached these three young ladies and asked them if they were all okay, and where had they been the previous evening, fishing to see who, if any, was not attached. Jenny, the quietest of the threesome, said she stayed in because she did not have a boyfriend. Very diplomatically I asked her if she would like to be introduced to my mate Luke. She agreed, so I said to leave it to me and I would fix it up.

Luke was delighted at the prospect and I suggested he write her a note introducing himself. He said he would like to but didn't know what to say, so I composed a letter which he copied verbatim.

A week later I arrived with Luke outside the Railwaymen's Club at the station, at the set time. It was a damp, dark winter's evening, when along came Jenny, bang on time. I introduced the pair and we went inside to have a drink. Well, from the first they got on like a house on fire. Up to this point, I didn't realise that Jenny was a vicar's daughter!

The relationship flourished and a couple of years later I accepted their wedding invitation. I must confess though, that I was a little disappointed that I was not asked to be best man. Never mind, it was a beautiful ceremony. They've been married several years now and have a young family and seem very happy together.

MEDLARS

One late Autumn Thursday, Ludo the foreman gave us a journey to shift some urgent cargo to the docks where a ship was loading, with the usual promise that we would be able to get away home early afterwards. Unfortunately, and beyond Ludo's con-trol, things went pear-shaped at teatime resulting in a ballast train being stranded some thirty miles away without a loco, as the train engine had been called upon to assist a failed passenger train. The ballast wagons were programmed to have been returned to the quarry this particular evening to be reloaded on the Friday for weekend engineering work. So we had little choice but to help Ludo out and be diverted after our last load into the docks, to go and fetch them.

We slipped down light engine, found the empties in the refuge. I coupled up, looked around the train and did a brake test, then returned to the signal post telephone and told the bobby that we were ready to depart. He apologised but said we would have to wait about two hours before he would be able to give us the road because the stopper, the milky, the mail, the express, and another stopper were on each other's tails and he couldn't give us a path, for there was no margin between them. My driver, Doug Peat, wasn't very impressed and told Ludo on the phone that he was most displeased, in language that cannot be repeated here. Ludo phoned our reticent signalman where we were holed up but it was useless. It was nightfall and we were finishing a can of tea when Doug said "any apple trees around here?"

"Not that I know of" I replied, "but down the embankment by the Up distant signal there's a Medlar tree."

"They'll do" said Doug.

Now Medlars are an old fashioned fruit and look something like pomegranates, and are just as awkward to eat, and you have to hang them in a shed for ages until they are practically rotten before you eat them.

So the fireman and I set off in the dark with one handlamp to try and locate this tree.

"It's about here" I said to Spike, as we struggled down the embankment, very overgrown these days, and reached the wire boundary fence, disturbing a lot of roosting woodpigeons as we went. I climbed over into the wood, followed by Spike. Unfortunate-ly as he arrived on the other side, one foot landed in a discarded PWay bucket used for grease, but now full of stinking water. He wasn't very impressed but I could not stop laughing at his predicament and the language was very impressive too. As I laughed, I turned around and scratched my face on a branch, causing my eye to run. We picked our Medlars and returned to the loco where Doug was waiting.

"What's the matter with your eye?" said Doug, "It's bleeding."

What I thought were tears was blood, no wonder it was so painful.

Eventually the bobby gave us the road when he saw there was sufficient time not to delay other traffic, and at length we deposited the empties and took the loco to shed.

Next morning I thought I'd better take my sore eye to the doctors, who prescribed some drops and advised me to sit in the dark for forty-eight hours. Hell to that, I thought, so I bought an eye patch from the chemist and went off to work at lunch time. Ludo would not allow me to book on duty because I now had restricted vision and told me to go home and do as the doctor had said and sit in the dark.

Forty-eight hours in the dark is a long time. No, I wouldn't like to be without my sight....

Nº 4468

UNWELCOMED GUESTS

Last month I was attending a meeting at Headquarters and the boss there was talking about staff absenteeism and the current 'flu epidemic. He's usually quite an amiable man, one of those old-fashioned people who was fifty on his twenty-first birthday, and we share a passion for collecting railway paraphernalia. During the course of this debate he announced that he had only been off sick **once** in twenty three years, with appendicitis. "H'mm" thought I, you've never pinched Medlars, caught German Measles off one of your young commuters, pulled a muscle struggling with ill-tempered swan's neck vacuum pipes, or been dragged face down along a platform with your dust coat trapped in a parcel van door!

First thing that morning I had a message that one of our signalmen had been taken ill and admitted to hospital. That particular box had a complement of four staff normally, but at the moment there were two vacancies due to promotions. Ellis Daniels had just resumed from sick leave after having a big toe amputated and now Gary Lander, coincidentally was in hospital, probably for the same operation. You can perhaps imagine the response of our relief signalman when I asked him to cover Gary's shift and explained why he had been admitted for similar surgery.

"It must be something in the carpet" he said, "better get Rentokil in."

Two boxes further down the line had had a problem with an adder back along in the summer, necessitating the Pest Control Officer being summoned, which had been the subject of conversation for a day or two at the time, with one or two additional comments added by various members of staff.

Some time ago during the summer I was working a branch passenger line, with all the windows open to the maximum, when - whilst passing through woodlands - an adder, obviously dislodged from a tree branch, was flung into the van and landed, rather stunned on the floor. I left it alone until we arrived at the next halt and then carefully picked it up and placed it in the bushes. It obviously recovered because on the next trip down the branch it was nowhere to be found on the platform.

EELING

Many of the local railwaymen were very keen fishermen. Ned Penn would catch eels on Thursday evenings to use for bait the following weekend. He was a guard and lived next door to Gossip Garters, but could Ned tell yarns! Middle-aged, stocky, with a very full head of swept-back white hair, he had some comical sayings and was prone to exagger-ating when telling a story. He would go to sea in his son's boat and had designed a form of spinner for mackerel fishing, developing the idea from a version he'd seen in another port. He called it his 'endless windless' and would go on for hours about it, egged on by fellow trainmen. He said once that he had caught a five pounds and **seventeen** ounce bass!

Come Thursdays, one of my cats seemed to know it was the night for eel supper and would raid Ned's tin bath for the shiny brutes and bring them home, one at a time, to eat. As often as I could I tried to rescue them and drop them into my garden pond but usually they would lie upside down and lifeless within the hour, my efforts wasted. Have you ever tried to pick a live eel up, it's a bit of a struggle, believe me!

Late Autumn, after the leaves have fallen, is the best time to clean out the fishpond and, if the pond is large it may mean you have to stand inside, after baling out the water, and ladle out the mud residue. There's nothing like the smell of pond-bottoms!

So that you do not damage the pond liner, bare hands are the best tools. I then had quite a shock to find a live eel that had survived the cat. How long it had been there I don't know, but later that very evening it found a new home in a local stream under the railway arches.

FISHING

Don Pears, the driver, also owned his own boat and would go out to sea for several miles with a couple of mates, usually after a few pints. He is a very shrewd fellow and seawise. If they were anchored out in the bay or beyond in the sea lanes and felt but one strange wave rock the boat in an otherwise calm sea, they would make for port immediately, taking this as an omen of a change in the weather, and time for a drink. Although he transported his boat around on a trailer, pulled by one of his mates, he never had a car himself and rode about the parish on an ancient scooter, and to the best of my knowledge has had 'L' plates up for the last thirty years.

For a change sometimes they would hitch the boat up and drive to the other coast, travelling for miles. One such night they had a very bountiful catch and put into a 'foreign' port, and when they came ashore they were jeered and jostled by the local fishermen who resented their intrusion. Usually the worse for drink, I'm sure they gave as good as they got!

One of the worst railway cargoes we had was mackerel, unfit for human consumption, that had laid for days on the quay and not even the seagulls would touch it. It was sent up north for processing into fertilizer. It would hum for miles and the awful smell from the slime that ran out of the coal wagon doors onto the couplings and brake pipes got onto your uniform. Usually the same wagons were returned a week later for reloading and were even riper. Where it dripped down onto the wagon undergear and onto the cast iron brake blocks and subsequently was heated by brake applications and part cooked, it was even worse.

One Monday evening I had to detach such a wagon from the middle of our train because it developed a 'hot box', the wheel bearing overheating. Next day the carriage and wagon department attended to it at this outstation and 'green carded' it for 'one journey only'. Twenty miles further up the line the same fault occurred again and I had to detach it once more en route and subsequently two days later stop and attach it again. I presume, because of its awful condition, the examiner had just topped the axle box up with oil on the first occasion and the oil pads had been left, causing the same fault to recur.

SEA HARVESTS

At least in steam days when the fish trains followed each other up the main in the evenings to a variety of destinations, you could only smell them for a few minutes after their passage, but it was never as bad as these trains, which left their smell behind in cuttings and stations for seemingly ages.

Another cargo from this particular dock is calcified seaweed, that is dredged from the roads around the estuary. This looks more like a very coarse sand and is also used for agricultural purposes. As late as 1985 they regularly used the steam shunter there, lifting the heavy traffic from the quayside into the transfer sidings, five wagons at a time, then forming it up into full length trains, ready to be collected in the evenings by a British Rail loco, when the branch passenger trains had gone to bed. As was common in later years the train guard had to perform all the shunting by himself, for economic reasons. I used to enjoy getting my hands dirty. Often the siding accommodation and run-around facilities were very limited after rationalisation post Dr Beeching. This means that you had two pints' worth of wagons and needed to get them all into a pint pot, hanging onto your empty inwards traffic, while you hauled out the loaded to form your train. Of course it was always dark and the sidings very overgrown with buddleia and fennel, something like playing draughts in the attic. Woe betide the guard who made an error and caused a double shunt! The driver would give him hell, a legacy I suppose from steam days when, as a fireman he would then have had to shovel another load of coal into the firebox.

WATERWAYS

Steam locos were everywhere when I first became a company servant, running alongside the diesels in the early sixties. Happily in more recent times we sometimes have a steam special run through our patch, and it is nice to be involved in some small capacity at least, in their running. This may mean manning a remote but photogenic location, perhaps at a level crossing, seeing that any would-be enthusiast does not end up inside the lifting barriers when they are lowered.

I did get a little egg on my face recently though, when 'The Duke' was booked into a loop on the Fen for a water stop under the wires with an enthusiasts' charter train. To me, taking water meant the fireman climbing atop the tender, lifting the manhole cover and dropping in the water bag. As this was to happen under the wires I raised the question of the safety of such an operation - did we need a temporary isolation?

A road tanker arrived at the scene and it was directed down the signal in anticipation and stopped where the loco tender would be brought to a stand. Right on time, the 'special' drew into the loop. I needn't have worried. All of us present there have now learned that these main line steam engines have a special connection under the footplate of the tender, and the tanker is connected up with high pressure hoses and the water transferred under pressure. Oh well, we know better now!

SHUNTING

Locomotive turntables were common throughout the railway system in order that steam tender engines could be turned around for their return journey and run chimney first. Tank engines, of course, ran just as often bunker first as chimney first.

In the very early days of railways, a lot of even small stations had turntables just of sufficient length to accommodate one wagon, to direct it from one running road into a siding for loading as an alternative to hand points, not requiring so much land area. From the turntable to its required position, either a shunting horse was employed or it was simply manhandled with an iron bar, levered under the wheels.

A lot of gravity shunting still goes on in some locations, especially those without run-around facilities, or it is often quicker to shunt in this manner. Approaching the desired siding on a downhill section the train is brought to a stand short of the points and the brakes secured. When safe to do so the locomotive, and perhaps those wagons not required at this location, are then sent ahead clear of the points. The shunter then releases all the automatic brakes, starting at the rear after the points have been set for the siding. Then, carefully controlling their acceleration under gravity, the shunter allows the wagon to roll forwards into the siding, clear of the points, before applying the handbrakes. An experienced man accomplished this in no time but anyone inexperienced or a bit nervous is very tempted to brake the rolling wagons pre-maturely and runs the risk of stopping them short and trapping the locomotive in. Special care is required with some vehicles, especially for some reason, continental ferry vans, whose handbrakes are notoriously inefficient and cannot be relied upon for braking purposes. Side-screw brakes can also be temperamental, sometimes the brake wheel seizes on, with grease and gunge.

Of course, sometimes the locomotive finishes up trapped by wagons that for one reason or another have halted prematurely and then initiative is called for to try and move them in clear. Sometimes a bar or shunting pole can be levered into the wagon's spokes to ease them forward, or a rope or chain attached from the loco draw bar to the leading wagon's coupling. At some locations it is possible to summon the assistance of the work's shunter with a tractor or other suitable road vehicle to move them. He'd seen it all before and never usually objected too strongly. If it is not possible to obtain such remedies, then an assisting loco has to be called for. By this time, the language is not very sweet all round, especially from the crew of the assisting loco thus summoned, delaying them in their other duties too. Already hot and bothered by causing this delay yourself and probably physically weary of trying to move the wagons unaided, the last thing you want is some verbal abuse and leg-pulling from yet another set of men!

SNOWMEN

Traincrews and yard staff are instructed from day one about the working of hand points and the necessity to check them each time they are operated to make sure the switch rail has moved fully and no gap left in the trailing end so that the flange of a vehicle does not intercede and deflect them, thus causing a derailment. During snow it always pays to take a handbrush, or stick, and clear the snow off of the slide-chairs before starting work, or else any left there compacts into ice, obstructing the switch rail from moving fully into position and causing problems. Points on the running lines are worked remotely by the signalman and have additional safety features to prove that they have operated fully with the detection and facing point locks working indepen-dently, thus proving to the signalman they have moved the full distance and have locked into position. At busy junctions a 'snowman' may be on duty, as necessary, to keep the points clear of ice and snow.

Troublesome locations have some form of automatic point heaters, worked usually by gas, that cuts in when the temperature drops below zero, thus keeping them free and safe.

When I was a signalman there was neither the luxury of a 'snowman' nor point heaters; even the box itself had calor gas lights and an Elsan loo, so when you had five-five-fived to the box in rear it paid to take the brush and sweep the slide rails yourself. Number six crossover was troublesome in cold weather, the rails contracting beyond the limit of the detection apparatus. We kept old rags and newspapers for such times, doused them in paraffin and placed them under the switch rail and set fire to them. It looked quite dramatic on a dark winter's morning for about ten minutes before the first train arrived - and it worked!

TURNTABLES

Most turntables disappeared after steam locos went but there are a few left at some locations and they are useful for turning power cars, necessary some-times when a defective vehicle is being replaced.

The turntable at my old depot has survived attempts by the railway to remove it and now has a preserv-ation order placed on it. It is still used occasionally to turn a diesel loco because diesels suffer excessive flange wear on one side due to an abundance of tight left hand curves in the district - turning the loco thus equalises this wear.

Not long ago all movements of engines required servicing by the fitters had to come onto shed via the turntable. A good driver would be capable of stop-ping the loco in exactly the right spot. A class forty six was very long and also weighed in at 139 tonnes so you needed the driver to be precise with his manoeuvring. As a second-man then turned the engine around, usually single-handed, by winding the table manually. It did have a vacuum powered motor but, by the time you had coupled the apparatus up to your engine and emptied its two large vacuum reservoirs, it was far quicker to perform the task manually. In later days one section of the table's round rail had a short uphill section, opposite number six road. This meant you needed to build up a bit of momentum as you approached it. Of course, once over the rise there was a down hill section and if you did not judge your winding accordingly going over the top the engine would run away under gravity and you missed your destined road, then it was necessary to stop, put the table into reverse gear and start winding again, usually accom-panied by a bit of abuse from your driver and heckling by the fitters!

In steam days, moving a dead loco onto the shed was an art in itself. Of course you could propel it into the table with another engine but you needed boiler pressure to drive it off. The shed pilot engine would therefore push and pull the engine up and down the depot yard with a man on its footplate to operate the reversing gear, then building up air pressure in the boiler. For some reason or other, locomotives hated this operation and would squeal and wheeze and complain bitterly during the whole procedure.

SWIMMING POOLS

At the lowest part of the turntable pit is a storm water drain that needs to be regularly cleaned of debris or else it fills up like a round swimming pool and then becomes a pig to empty.

During that very hot summer of 1976 I spent a lot of time on a regular freight turn and if traffic was very light we would bring along our swimming trunks and towels. There were two places where it was possible to take the waters. The first option was the river by the second level crossing, where a weir damned back the cold dark waters to sufficient depth for swimming, or second choice was the town's baths. At the first location, at Friday lunchtimes, the water bailiff's wife baked yeast buns in her Rayburn and if you were lucky she would bring out a brown paper bag full for the train crew. They were delicious, straight out of the oven.

One day, we elected to stop adjacent to the town's baths, shut down the loco, applied plenty of hand-brakes and nipped in for a quick dip. After a pleasant half-hour we decided we'd had enough and made for the changing room - a very basic affair consisting of four wooden benches and two dozen coat pegs. All the train crew had come prepared, but scruffy Bert Hoblin, the shunter, had forgotten and swam in his grubby 'Y'-fronts.

In the changing room stands Bert, no towel, so he helps himself to one off the peg. I can see him now, sat down wrapped in the borrowed towel, trying to pull his socks on over his wet feet. But look out! - dripping wet - a large fellow comes in and cannot find his towel. He then sees our Bert. Needless to say we all made a very quick exit and finished dressing on the train!

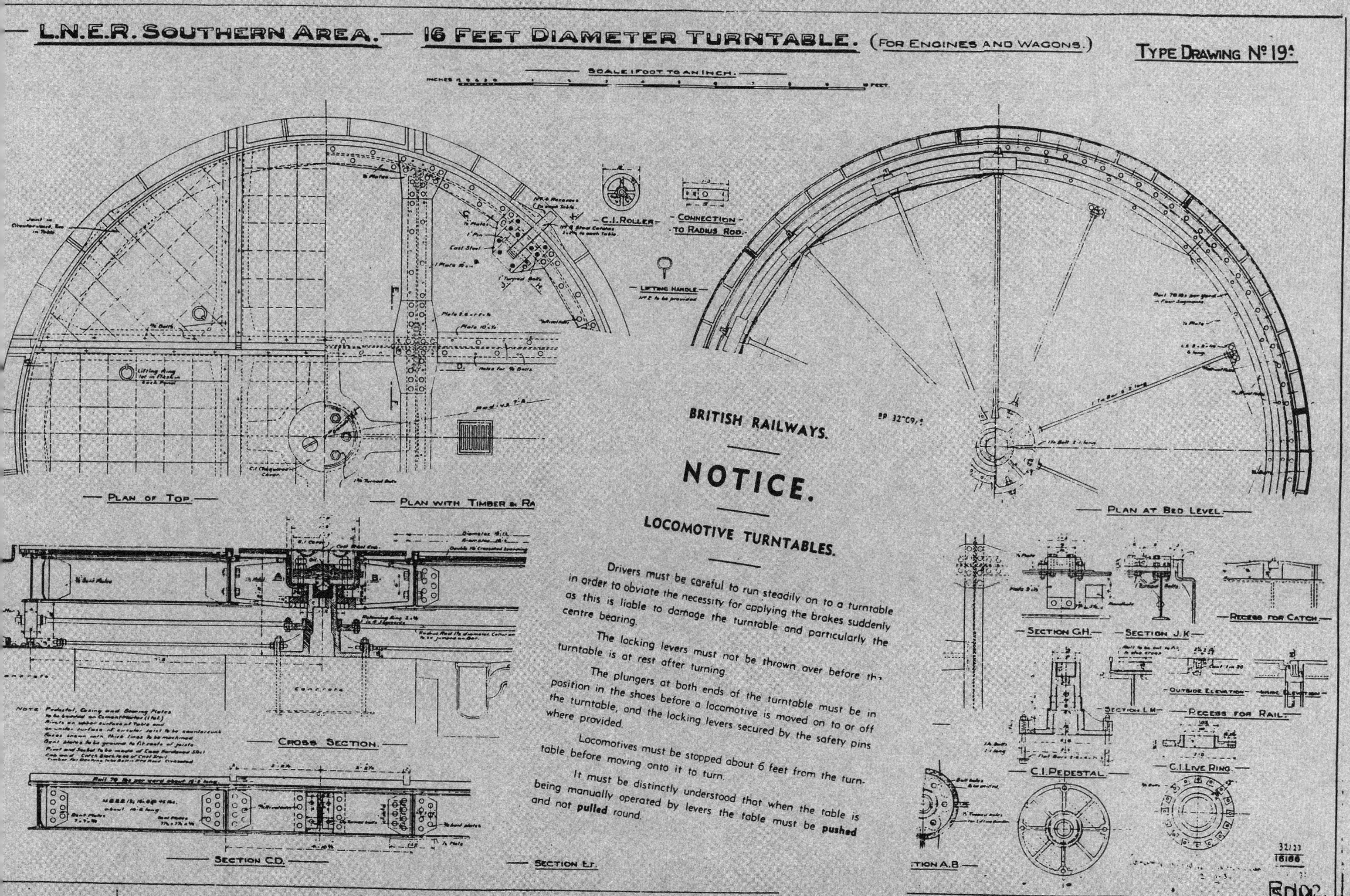

BRITISH RAILWAYS.

NOTICE.

LOCOMOTIVE TURNTABLES.

Drivers must be careful to run steadily on to a turntable in order to obviate the necessity for applying the brakes suddenly as this is liable to damage the turntable and particularly the centre bearing.

The locking levers must not be thrown over before the turntable is at rest after turning.

The plungers at both ends of the turntable must be in position in the shoes before a locomotive is moved on to or off the turntable, and the locking levers secured by the safety pins where provided.

Locomotives must be stopped about 6 feet from the turntable before moving onto it to turn.

It must be distinctly understood that when the table is being manually operated by levers the table must be **pushed** and not **pulled** round.

STRATEGIC RESERVES

Did you ever ponder, on a pleasant Sunday afternoon whilst walking along a disused railway line, feeling somewhat uneasy, or unexplained guilt, not alone, why such locations, as opposed to others, had not yet gone under the plough?

Do you recall in the sixties and seventies several articles appearing in enthusiasts' magazines about the 'Strategic Reserves of Steam Locomotives?' I strongly believe that these Reserves do still exist, neglected and forgotten nowadays, in several rural locations. You cannot help but feel whilst picking your way through the undergrowth along old track beds, that around the next curve you will come across a secret hoard of locomotives, stored away by some Government Department, along with sufficient spares, that could be used in a future war should our island become blockaded. In these articles sufficient evidence was not presented to imply that large numbers of locomotives had apparently disappeared without trace, not recorded as ever having reached the various scrap yards of the period. I think it was suggested that some two hundred and fifty locomotives were never accounted for.

So keep on with your Sunday afternoon walks along our abandoned railroads. One day you may discover one such Reserve. At least there are enough technical skills, know-how and expertise on our island's preserved railways to man at least a very basic railway in a time of crisis...

Track Access Arrangements -
broad gauge days!.

SLUDGE AND DUST

Generally speaking the boilers on steam locos were washed out every ten days, to remove all the residue and deposits after evaporating several thousand gallons of water, and the various regions had laid down procedures for ensuring this job was done regularly. Our depot did this mucky job when the last digit of the loco number coincided with the day's date. If, for example, the last digit was six, the loco had a washout on the sixth, sixteenth and twenty-sixth of the month. The amount of sludge and silt varied in different areas depending on the quality of water available, and a build up of this material made the boiler inefficient, sometimes priming.

You might recall seeing a 'bright spot' on a loco's smoke box door, which was where the paint had been burnt off and the bared metal sported a coat of rust. A build up of sooty char and fine unburnt coal dust was deposited at the smoke box door end, and sometimes this itself would catch fire, scorching the paintwork. It was a filthy job shovelling this char out each day when the loco came to shed for servicing. Likewise the grate would need cleaning and raking to remove all the clinker, over the shed pits. I've had several loads of these spent materials and used them on a base for paths and driveways, where they provided an excellent foundation again, the quality of deposit and residue depended to some extent on the quality of the coal and its originating area.

More than once I have heard tell of the older men saying the coal atop the tender of the Royal Train had all been painted white!

ANNOUNCEMENTS

Heading on the Down road out of King's Cross yesterday, a very cheerful and pleasant Geordie conductor was adding his own comments to the script he was supposed to read during his announcements. I always found that if you added a few comments of your own on the public address system on board the train or with platform announcements, they would be appreciated by the public, especially the regulars who got bored hearing the same announcements every day. Sometimes some wit would 'phone the trains announcer and ask for a public announcement to be made that was designed to cause a smile.

"Would Mr Hugh Janus please report to the ticket office for a message?"

"If there is an A Roma on the platform meeting the 11.30 arrival, etc, etc."

One conductor at least on the Western became renowned for his off-the-cuff remarks.

"Ladies and gentlemen, we are now approaching Liskeard - Liskeard - any landlubbers requiring a service to Looe, please leap off here."

"Ladies and gentlemen, we are now approaching Saltash and the county boundary - I would like to advise you that it is against Common Market regulations to take Cornish Pasties out of the county without written authority, and to avoid embarrassment you are respectfully asked to hand these to the train crew immediately."

Peter, who used to work the Peterborough trains, announced regularly:

"We are now approaching Stamford, please change here for the pubs and churches."

The hostelry is five minutes from the last station and some evenings, when it was very hot, my mate would persuade me to go for a shandy during our meal break. If one of our passengers had used the card and booked in, there would be a couple of shandies waiting on the bar for us. Later, you would see these folk again during the course of the week and they would sometimes go out of their way to say a special 'thank you' for your help. You could suggest that it would be a very good idea to buy a Weekly Explorer ticket, or that Petermouth was excellent for a day out and that there was a special daily excursion fare, which was all excellent business for the railway.

One night we were running late and Mad Mitch said we would still make time for a pint, he would therefore show me a short cut they used to use in steam days. Hell, we tried this route but I don't think anyone had been that way since the sixties and we had to fight our way through the brambles to find an exit. Unfortunately I caught my undercarriage on the fence wire as we climbed over, and that ruined by break completely!

"Stamford Town, change here for the pubs and churches."

PERKS

When the shop sales were on in Petermouth you could presume that a pair of thirty-year-olds that had just got on at a branch station at about 10am, had just taken their children to the school gates and were off in search of a few bargains. As you approached you could surprise them by saying first:

"Two cheap day returns to Petermouth?"

Somewhat bemused they would usually say:

"Yes please, but how did you know where we are going?"

One guard used to reply:

"A bit of fresh lipstick and a clean pair of drawers usually means Petermouth!"

That usually broke the ice and set them off to a good start to their day.

Now one such pair remembered this guard and next morning returned and presented him with a flash new cigarette lighter. He was very grateful for their kindness but daren't take it home with him or else he would have faced an inquisition from his partner. It so happened that another guard, Larry Kirk, had lost his lighter that very morning, so the first guard passed it on, with a twinkle in his eye, and told him about the lipstick ladies!

About this time, Larry was booked to work his first Royal Train, but on the very morning woke up with a bad dose of German Measles, had to report sick, and was therefore very disappointed. Anyhow, the guard who was then rostered vice Larry kept his old mate in mind and borrowed a nice crisp white towel and a couple of rolls of posh loo paper from the Train, which he presented to him by way of compensation. Larry had been an upholsterer and carpet layer before he joined the railway, and paid his mate back in kind at a later date.

DAD'S ARMY

I have mentioned several times that the locomen often had part time jobs in the fifties and sixties to supplement their wages. During the seventies an agreement was reached between the unions, the men, and the Permanent Way Department, that permitted traincrew, if they so desired, to join the relaying gangs on Sundays and make a shilling, even though at this time drivers had a ban on rest day working. At our depot, such volunteers were known as 'Dad's Army'.

One Guard Lampshire, who was a bit of a character, used to go along and work with them on the shovel, but he was a bit of a skiver and always volunteered to go and put the kettle on and make a brew, when the chance permitted. At this time, the men still used to use the cabins, spaced about a quarter of a mile apart, all along the line. During the winter the first man to get into the hut would arrange to obtain a seat by the open fire, upon which the old blackened cast iron kettle would be singing. Over a cup of tea and a smoke, many yarns would be told of the old days. Now Guard Lampshire had to have the last say when it came to tales of his conquests and told of his efforts in the last war, on how he had contracted a 'Full House' out in the East during military service.

"What do you mean, a 'Full House'? one youngster interrupted.

"Syphilis, gonorrhea and crabs, all at the same time" he boasted.

"Take him off the cooking" said the ganger.

And that was the last time Lampshire ever made tea for the gang.

‘During rain, wind and snow,
into the cabin we must go!’

CHEAP AND CHEERFUL

One of our branches ran across county and served a few old mining villages and one particularly had seen better days. Even the regulars from there seemed to be perpetually in a run-down state. The children all wore hand-me-downs or jumble sale clothes, and the young maidens wore cheap and cheerful boutique fashions.

A couple of families in particular used the line for shopping, collecting their dole, trips to the doctors, and one of these families used to go to Mass on Sunday mornings during the summer months' opening.

The father of this Catholic family was a veritable character, and looked a comic through and through. He was very short, middle-aged since his thirties, always wearing a dirty white mac, had a red nose and a roll-up perpetually hung from his top lip. On Saturday nights during the summer season he would carry his accordion along on the train, which was only seemingly inches shorter than his good self. He would go around the town's pubs and play and dance a jig. Now I am tone deaf but could perceive that either he or his instrument was severely out of tune.

One Wednesday morning in later times, his oldest son joined the train at this station, but remarkably was going in the Up direction, carrying a cheap plastic sports holdall and wearing a brand new pair of black and white trainers.

"Aye, aye" says I, "what's on then, where are you off today?"

By now we were a couple of miles further along the line.

"Guernsey", he replied excitedly, and searched for his tickets.

Then he almost burst into tears and exclaimed:

"I've left them on the kitchen table!"

I hurried through the train to speak to my driver, explained the predicament, and he immediately stopped, and with me in the back cab set back to the station. Whilst the boy ran home to collect the tickets, I explained to the handful of passengers what had happened and reassured them they would make their connections okay at the Junction.

Five minutes later we were on our way again, and arrived on the main line right time. Both his grateful parents came and thanked me the following morning.

WILDLIFE

Most of the time at work was spent travelling out in the countryside, in all the seasons, at all hours and in all weathers, and it was nice to sit back and watch the years go by, along with all the wildlife.

At one branch halt, on the bank to the north of the station, there was a colony of foxes that paid little heed to the passage of the trains, just pausing in the shadows as we went back and forth throughout the day. In the early spring it was always a delight to see the cubs at play. Not everyone was so delighted though. I picked up a little old lady one early summer morning at this halt, where she had been waiting alone for the train. She spoke very fearfully when I went to check her ticket and said "I've just seen some wolves" and she was visibly in a state of shock!

At the same time as we saw the cubs, the first primrose of the year would be appearing at the next station, Hag Town, as American Servicemen called it during the last war, and we would look for them from late February onwards. The first wild flowers, of course, are the snowdrops which appear abundantly in the damp and sheltered hedge bottoms.

Whilst working one November night out in the 'styx' on an engineering train, the spine-chilling call of a vixen and dog fox could be heard each time there was a pause in the wail and clatter of the track machines. Nothing, I believe, is so atavistic as the fox in the mating season.

I'd like a pound for every time we've stopped a freight train or light engine, climbed over the fence and walked across a meadow to upright a sheep on its back. Always it is a surprise to see how quickly a sheep is defeated and dies, once it is upside down. If you were not quick enough during hot dry days the crows would get in first and attack their eyes and blind them, in their search for moisture.

One or two of our tracks ran, for their greater length, along the river banks and it was not uncommon to see as many as five kingfishers on at least one trip, and you could prepare a discerning passenger where to look out for them. We managed to glimpse an otter on one occasion.

Driver Dennis Greenhouse once showed me a kingfisher's nest hole on the river bank, by the viaduct, near to where Ludo's unit had failed. Dippers are very common in the streams here too, as well as the herons. At the heads of most of the valleys a pair of buzzards can be seen, circling their great gyres, mewing as they turned, lording over their various kingdoms.

I have to confess I shall always be a country boy at heart.....

"That bloody sign wasn't there last
August when we came blackberrying."

SPOILS

If we collided with a pheasant often we'd stop immediately, or at least on our return journey, and pick it up for the table. Being a vegetarian this never appealed to me but one day whilst working a short engineers' train to the Junction, I observed a pheasant whirl away into the undergrowth by the motorway bridge after flying into our loco. After detaching our train in the yard, we were to return light engine to our depot, so I told the driver what had happened. We slowed to a walking pace adjacent to the bridge and found the poor pheasant sitting in the cess, alive, unmarked, but obviously suffering internal injuries. I carefully picked it up and asked the driver if he would pull its neck and end its suffering. Neither he nor his mate could do this, so I had no choice but to take it with us and find a vet. I sat in the back cab of the loco with the bird cradled on my lap. It struggled once or twice during the journey but eventually after heavily soiling my trousers gave up the ghost. After we arrived back on shed the driver was only too willing to relieve me of the carcass for Sunday's dinner.

Often when we were turned into a loop line with freight to give priority to an express we'd hop over the fence and harvest a flat-bowl cabbage, a turnip or apples - a practice of trainmen from the dawn of the railway age. An old driver once told me not to worry about it because the farmer, like his father and grandfather before, always tilled the row next to the railway anyway.

In the late summer we'd pick blackberries and take them home in our tea cans. You may have noticed that several apple trees grow on the railway banks, seeded by discarded apple-cores over the years. With experience came the knowledge of the best types to go with your blackberries. In early Autumn we'd often stop the first branch trains of the morning and gather mushrooms in our caps from old horse pastures, and were joined sometimes by a passenger or two, who were only too pleased for the opportunity and didn't complain if we were a minute or two down at the destination stations!

NIGHT SHIFTS

As the main lines of the railway system ran continuously for twenty four hours a day this meant that you had to do your share of night work. Until recent times, staff on a week of night duty received additional payment by way of incentive to cover anti-social hours spent away from home.

One hot summer Sunday I spent the whole of my shift as a guard on a tunnel-cleaning train. The trackmen, lying on the top of specially modified vans, using ordinary grass rakes, scraped the soot from the tunnel roof as the train very slowly drew through the tunnel. You can imagine, perhaps, the dust and fumes we had to endure. Because we spent the whole of the day within the tunnel, we were paid night rate for the shift.

Most of the night shift, when not engaged on other tasks of duty, tend to sit and read during the small hours to help pass away the time and stay awake. I sometimes used to occupy this time to best advantage between my various tasks, to draw or write:

> "Are there ghosts in the station's, dark shadows, sepulchral, deep, dismal, cheerless? I fancy there might well be, though in truth I never mind the company of souls lost in transit between Earth Mother and stellar space.
> Generations of railwaymen down a century and a half here toiled for long hours.
> Soldiers went to their last wars, bid farewells to unfaithful wives - indifferent mothers.
> Children, too. Parted and departed.
> Many tears are still swept away each evening from under the stations' dim canopies.
> Love and lovers lost - unrequited.
> The desperate - lonely and unheard - life ended in the four foot. Ghosts, mice and moths in the stations' shadows. I oft feel their presence."